FROM BUST TO BANK STEP BY STEP GUIDE TO PET SITTING BUSINESS

Soham M.

Copyright © 2018

All rights reserved. No part of this book may be reproduced or transmitted in any form or by any means, electronic or mechanical, including photocopying, recording or by any information storage and retrieval system without written permission of the publisher, except for the inclusion of brief quotations in a review.

Disclaimer:

Please read the Disclaimer carefully before you read this book. You accept and agree to be bound and abide by the Disclaimer. The information contained on this book is for educational and informational purposes only. The information contained on this book is not intended as, and shall not be understood or construed as, professional advice.

The brand names or logos discussed in this book are property of their respective owners.

Why Pet Sitting Business? 5
Legal Requirements 7
Pet Sitting Is Not Dog Walking 10
Avoiding The Dangers 12
Planning For Expansion 14
Creating An Offer 16
Importance Of Testimonials 18
Getting Your Clients 20
Utilizing Power Of Flyers Correctly 23
Pitfalls To Avoid 25
What To Offer 26
The Power Of Videos 28
Interacting With First Time Clients 29
The Importance Of Sales Script 31
Pricing 32
Promotions 34

Why Pet Sitting Business?

There is no better time to start a pet sitting business especially if you love the company of animals. This business offers a lucrative business opportunity for those passionate pet lovers.

The book is written with the objective to help you understand the pros and cons of a pet sitting business. While this book isn't a comprehensive guide, it will help you kick-start the business of pet sitting.

You as a pet sitter might work as an independent contractor, but if you form a firm to represent your business then you need to register your company with the state. The registration grants a legal status to the business. Though the licensing requirements vary from state to state, thus it is advisable to check in your respective states for obtaining the license. Now a day every state has its website, and you can check the state government's website to determine the type of license required for pet sitting business. These websites also have information on the documents required for obtaining a license for pet sitting business.

Legal Requirements

Many people mix up the business registration and license, both serve different purposes. While registration gives a legal status to the business, a license is required if the business is termed as hazardous. The pet sitting business involves dealing with animals, walking them in the park, poses threat to the general public, hence the license ensures that the business is abiding by the laws and generally builds trust. Procuring the license might involve certain expenses; again the fees charged by the states vary.

Pet sitting as a business also require that the business must be properly insured. Insurance ensures protection from financial, legal or accidental damages. Pets could be injured, or they can inflict injuries to the pet sitter or anyone from the public, hence it is necessary to obtain insurance. The premium for pet sitting business is quite affordable because generally it is believed to carry a lesser risk. You can check the quotation for the insurance online through their websites and even compare their plans, so you can select the best one for you. A Pet sitting business also require a bond, usually, the bond is executed between three parties, and the premium for surety bonds are a one time expense. Surety bonds are basically an instrument to transfer the risk involved in the business. The objective of a surety bond is to protect the public from third-party risk, which in this case is a pet.

You might be required to obtain a surety bond before applying for the license or you might be required to obtain the bond later. Surety bonds usually have to be paid yearly, you must check with your insurance company. Generally, insurance companies charge anywhere between 1% - 15% depending upon the business, for example, if your company charges 2% premium on $10,000, then the yearly premium amounts to $200. Surety bonds serve as a legal guarantee that the business will abide by the state and federal laws.

A Pet sitting business is a business entity is also required to pay regular taxes, if your business plans to hire people then it has to classify the employees, the business itself can be classified as an independent contractor business. An employee working with the company does not have to worry about the taxation part because the company deducts the amount of tax before paying the salary, in your case, your customer might not care to deduct the tax, hence the liability for paying tax falls on you. It would be advisable to maintain regular records of income and expenses to avoid any hassles with authorities later. An expense incurred for business is generally written-off against the business income. If you maintain proper records of the expenses, then you can claim the write-off of such expenses. A pet sitting business would usually incur expenses on the phone, office, buying pet supplies and flyers, etc.

If you are starting as a business then it is advisable to have a proper business card with a logo. A website might not be necessary at the initial stage because when you build a website, your business area becomes quite vast, and if you do get a business enquiry from an area that you don't service, then it might become embarrassing for you to turn the client down.

Pet Sitting Is Not Dog Walking

Many people confuse pet sitting business as dog walking. Both are different, a person who walks the dog might walk multiple dogs at a time, a pet sitters job is much more demanding because he has to deal with pets as well as their owners. A pet sitter has to be aware of the pet's health history, health issues, and the medications and have to be tactful while dealing with them. A pet might require watering or playing or both. Every pet has different nutritional requirements. A pet sitter is not just someone who takes care of pets; he is the primary caregiver of the pet. The biggest requirement for a pet sitter is his love for animals; if you find animals creepy then it is better to stay away from the business. The pet sitting might not involve dogs only; you might have to deal with a cat or a parakeet or worse an iguana. You must be willing to work with the animals, understand their behavior, and take care of them. Animals are beautiful creatures, and their needs are different. A pet sitting business cannot be started just for the sake of money, you, as a pet sitter must truly love the animals that are under your care. As a pet sitter, you must decide if you are comfortable making on-site visits, or you insist on your facility, there are people who might ask you to take the pet to the vet, some clients might ask you to stay overnight at their house. There are several issues that you must decide beforehand because your business if it is not defined clearly can cause confusion, and the image of your company might suffer.

A business, be it the pet sitting or a construction firm, thrives on a communication. If you are meeting a customer for the first time, then your customer might want to know everything about you and your business. Pets are like children for their owners, and they would like to see how their pets react to you and how you respond to their pets. It is very important to build a trust between both parties. A possible customer will demand references, certification, and your experience dealing with pets. It is advisable to keep everything ready; this issue is dealt separately later.

Avoiding The Dangers

However lucrative the pet sitting business might appear, it is fact that many people are forced to wind up the business within two years due to several factors, undercharging is the biggest culprit in the failure of the business. In their enthusiasm to get more clients, people resort to price cutting, they charge do little that it becomes difficult to sustain a viable business. Another mistake people often make is to accept clients that are far away. You must first focus on the local market and gradually expand the business. In their bid to expand rapidly, people begin to work haphazardly, enthused by the good response, they begin to hire people, take on the jobs that are difficult to manage. This lack of discipline and organization leads to confusion, and eventually closure of the business. The burning of cash is another area of concern, as soon as there is an inflow of business enquiries, people tend to go overboard, and begin spending on treats, free gifts to attract and retain customers. This must be avoided, the cash must be used for expansion of business, and a reasonable buffer must be maintained for unforeseen circumstances due to the unpredictable nature of the business.

The success of any business lies in patience and being organized. If you expect the business to be successful from day one then it might end up in disappointment. A business needs to be nurtured, given an opportunity to grow. If you don't rely on the business income for a year or so, you can expect to harvest rich rewards later on.

Planning For Expansion

As a businessman, you must plan for the expansion and recruitment of employees in advance. If you plan to recruit employees then you must follow this section. Employees, both contractual and a permanent can be recruited through online job sites, placing an advertisement in local newspapers. The hiring is a gradual process, typically you will not be recruiting people en masse, and the hiring will depend on the expansion of your business. Also, you must have a clearly defined role for an employee that aligns with your organization's vision.

If your business is expanding, it is a good sign, but you must carefully plan the recruitment process, in this way you will have ample time to select the candidates that could prove to be the assets of the company. It is completely normal to experience some anxiety when are hiring for the first time. However, the hiring also requires that you, as an entrepreneur must be aware of certain laws because you don't want any problems on the legal front. The most important step is to classify if you are hiring the person as an employee or independent contractor. It could be that you may not require the full-time employee, but the misclassification between an employee and an independent contractor could have grave ramifications.

The important thing to remember here is that before you can hire people for your business, you must apply for EIN or Employer Identification Number. This is mandatory because it helps the income tax department to ascertain whether the tax obligations are fully met. Once you have obtained EIN, you can apply for employee withholding tax.

Another important thing to consider while hiring an employee is to make sure that you are hiring a person who is eligible to work your country. Each new employee is required to sign firm I-9 along with the required documents. After you complete the above formalities, you can issue a job offer letter which spells the job description along with terms of employment. As your business grows, you will also require a payroll provider to maintain regular records.

Creating An Offer

The biggest mistake a pet sitting business owner makes is to offer each service as a product. While it is true that a service like a dog walking, giving medications to the pet or bathing the pet and trimming their nails are different products, selling them individually will make it look like you are exploiting the poor pet for your commercial gains. Instead, you must create an offer that looks lucrative to the pet owner, for example, you can put in the flyer that if the customer avails of your pet service by so and so day, and if they book three services, they might get bathing and nail trimming for free. While creating the offer, you can mention the price of bathing and nail trimming, this helps the customer to see the value he is getting by grabbing the offer. As a business owner, your focus must be on selling the offer. It would be difficult to compete in a competitive market by focusing on products alone. You must be familiar with last minute offers or Today Only offers, these types of offers have different products bundled together which offer substantial discounts. These offers compel your customers to take action. It creates a feeling of being left out. You must have noticed this trend on online websites too where a product that is priced

$1000 is priced at $795 if it is purchased right now. An offer always tells the story, for example instead of a simple pet sitting, why not offer a complete pet care solution that offers pet sitting, taking care of the medications, taking the pet to the vet if they have an appointment, bathing them. The possibilities are endless. This tells the customer that his pet is getting complete care and he can relax. The advantage to you as an entrepreneur is that a customer who was looking to book your service for taking their pet to the vet might end up buying other services too. While creating an offer, always focus on the benefits provided by the offer. The customer is more interested in benefits, and most businesses tend to advertise the features of their service. Instead on focusing on a problem, focus on providing a solution. While creating an offer always focus on the fear of losing an attractive offer. It is a human tendency to want what others want, by putting a time limit or numbers to your offer, you are invoking the sense of urgency in the buyer. They are bound to take quick action which eventually will lead to an increase in your business.

Importance Of Testimonials

You must combine various sales methods to attract your customer, however, if you don't have testimonials, your marketing campaign, however, brilliant might look pale. The customer who is visiting you for the first time isn't impressed by your tall claims, glossy marketing campaigns, or your attractive facility; he looks for signs of trust, and testimonials are the right tools to gauge the success of claims made by the business. Each customer has their own reasons for contacting your company, but they all have one concern in common, the satisfaction index of customers. If you have very few customers talking about you, it means that your customer satisfaction index is poor. Remember that happy customers translate into happy businesses. You must always strive to get a testimonial from a customer, if you can get a video testimonial, it would be great. Videos have the power to attach emotional value and they directly appeal to the emotions of your prospective customer. Testimonials act as a sales representative whose persuading power cannot be underestimated. A customer will always look at business or its claims with suspicion because whatever a company says, it has its vested interest in it. A testimonial has the power to answer the questions that might linger in the mind of your prospective customer; it reduces the anxiety in the mind of your prospective customer. Testimonials also serve as a powerful social proof; it gives unparallel power to the marketer.

Getting Your Clients

Pet sitting business strives on word of mouth. People who own the pets do not treat them as animals; pets are an integral part in the lives of the people. A pet sitter has to be trustworthy hence; pet sitting business requires a different strategy.

You must regularly visit dog parks; this is a place where you will meet people who own dogs. Networking is crucial the success of the business. You focus must be to make as many friends as possible. Try to help people who are walking with dogs, Don't do everything with a commercial interest. When you help people taking care of their pets, you demonstrate your authority in pet sitting business; this also shows that you are willing to travel the extra mile in your business. This helps to build trust, and even if you don't get immediate business, you can be sure of referrals coming your way. Always focus on good service, money will follow. Think of pets as a baby, ask yourself, are you willing to entrust your baby in the care of a stranger? This is the dilemma many pet owners face when hiring a pet sitter.

Many people rush to get business, and they rely on commercial websites, apps to get business. The problem with these websites and apps is that the competition is constantly growing and prices tend to drift lower as more people enter the pet sitting business. The commercial websites treat a business as a commodity, the prices are standardized, there is very little room for extra efforts because these websites charge a fat commission for referring a business, and this lowers the income of a pet sitter who is interested in making maximum money in a span of 12 hours or so. Hence, a personal approach with a long-term goal will reap handsome financial rewards as you build your reputation and delight your customers with unparalleled service.

You must be passionate about your business. Another way to get a potential customer is to offer first sitting or two for free. Free trial offers shows that you are passionate about your business, it shows your love for the animals and assures the people that their favorite pet is in safe hands. If it is uneconomical for you to offer free sittings, you can ask for transportation charges. This is the best way to stand out among your competition. Whatever you do, if you think only on commercial lines, if only profit is your motive then you might find that fighting competition is an uphill task.

Another way of obtaining clients is to set-up a Facebook page. You can join various pet lovers groups on Facebook. Start contributing articles, helpful tips in a group. If somebody needs help, you must be willing to offer help. Your contribution must be visible. The more you contribute, the better your chances of establishing yourself as an authority. If you want consistent business, you have to establish yourself as an authority.

Utilizing Power Of Flyers Correctly

You can also distribute flyers; however, the best place to distribute flyers is to meet the veterinary doctors and hospitals, be sure to offer some treats to the staff at the hospital. Many people distribute free treats for pets; this could be viewed with suspicion, it could also pose a risk to the hospital because if a pet falls ill or experiences some adverse reaction then you could lose the sympathy and support of the hospital forever. You can also visit shops selling pet items, and talk to them to put a flyer in the shop. You can also distribute the flyers directly to the people, but as mentioned previously, the best way to attract a customer is to offer a free sitting. People hate the idea of being stalked for commercial purposes. If you can demonstrate your passion for work, there are chances of you succeeding in a big way.

You can also visit the high rise apartments and try to contact the owners; however this might be difficult at first because the concierge might not allow such cold commercial approach, but if you visit the nearest park to those high rises, then there is a chance that you might find a group of customers. The people in high rise apartments are well-settled, lead a busy life, and are always on a lookout for someone whom they can trust to take care of their animals. You can also convince the concierge to allow you to put your flyers near the mailboxes of people. There is no substitute for dedication and hard work.

Pitfalls To Avoid

Many people build flashy websites, spend money on promotion and eventually shut the shop because a website is not required in the initial stages; it attracts too many people who would be from far-flung areas that would be uneconomical for you to service. While spending money on promoting a website, if a client contacts you from a far-flung area, and if you are unable to service the client, you can imagine the blow your reputation as a business owner could receive. When starting a business, always focus on nearby neighborhoods where you can provide prompt and efficient service. Once you become established, and you can afford a decent staff, you can spend money on websites and digital marketing.

What To Offer

You must prepare the list of services you offer for pets. Some people talk about themselves, their experience while designing the flyers, while this may work, but building trust is something that requires personal interaction. In the meantime, you can advertise the services provided by you. Some of the services that can be offered are:

Providing pets with their meals, and serving fresh water
Walking or playing with pets
Scooping the litter box and waste disposal
Brushing the pets

You can also offer to water the indoor plants and take out the trash
Some people might ask you to administer vitamins, while this might sound OK, the medication part must be properly discussed and mentioned in the contract.
Some people might demand that their dogs must be taken to walk without a leash. However, you must not agree to such demands and explain in a polite voice that thing was not possible because you not only care for the safety of their dog but care for the safety of other people, pets in the park. If you

walk a dog without a leash, you could lose your insurance.

You can also allocate a certain time for shelters walking dogs, this might not bring immediate clients but it goes a long way in building the trust. Just an hour or two every day might do wonders for your business because after providing service for few weeks, you can obtain a testimonial from the shelter, such testimonials will work wonders for your business.

The Power Of Videos

You can also record some videos of pet sitting that you have done. You will be able to show how much a pet enjoys your company. Videos can be a great way to establish you as an authority. If you have joined Facebook groups, you can post your videos in such groups. This will also help you build trust fast. Usually, people have photographs to show and post on social media groups, not many people record the videos of the pet care. You can also offer one video a month of their pet while it is with you. This could be an added service offering and once you implement it; you can expect positive results for your business. If you are keen on showing photographs then show pictures of you in other people's house, this will help you create an image of a trustworthy person.

Interacting With First Time Clients

A typical dog owner might ask you questions like what breeds of dogs have you walked/sit. What qualification do you hold for a pet sitting business? He might also be concerned about the insurance, he might also ask you about various training methods and would like to know if you have undergone any training, if you cannot provide satisfactory answers to the above questions, it could jeopardize your business prospects. If you can provide satisfactory answers then you might have landed a long-term prospect, you might even consider demonstrating your knowledge about the canine behavior. All these things go a long way in building trust in your ability to handle their beloved pets.

I would highly recommend you get some certifications from reputed pet associations. While this may not be necessary but as a businessman, you must keep in mind that customers love working with professionals, they do not want to hand over their pet to an unqualified person. Try to build better relations with vets; if possible you can agree to distribute their visiting cards or brochures to prospective clients. A recommendation from a vet goes a long way in boosting your brand value. You can also visit pet grooming stores in your locality and explore mutually beneficial relationships.

The Importance Of Sales Script

Before venturing out to talk to your prospective clients, it would be best if you prepare a two-minute sales script and practice it every day, if you cannot have a friend to pose as a dummy customer, you can practice the sales script in front of the mirror. Try to practice your sales script in front of as many friends as possible; you are going to feel very uncomfortable doing all this. Initially, you will feel awkward. You can also have someone shoot the video while you are giving a presentation. This will help you to improvise your body language. This will help you become more confident. The process of growth is never going to be comfortable; you have to step out of your comfort zone. If you feel worse doing the above, it means you are moving in the right direction.

Pricing

Pricing is extremely important if you want to survive long-term in the business. A good business model would be the one where customers and business discover the best price that makes them both happy.

You can price your consultation fee at $10. Usually, this is the first time you visit the prospective client to discuss pet sitting. You can also charge by the number of visits, many pet sitting businesses charge by the number of pets, if you are looking to build a loyal customer base, then your pricing must provide delight to the customer. You can also offer progressive discounts, for example, if one visit costs $30, then two visits can be offered for $25 each, and three visits at $20 each. Such progressive discounts ensure that customers book your services for a longer period and thus result in higher revenues. Your pricing must also include scooping of poops/cleaning of litter boxes at no additional charge. Your focus must be to set the benchmark in the industry even if it means moving away from the conventional practices. If a client asks you to visit only for cleaning the poops, then you can charge them your normal visit charges. You can derive multiple products from a single product, for example, if you are sitting a pet; you can also offer to clean their beds, cages at a nominal price and the owners would not mind paying a little extra for complete care solution for their beloved pets. Usually, medications should be charged per pet, and not on per medication. The entire activity of your business must focus on customer delight. Many people charge for providing updates on email or over text message, you must strive to provide additional services like this for free.

Promotions

You can also reach out to the local walkers in your area. If there is an assignment that they don't want to take, they can always refer those clients to you. You can also help them if they need your help occasionally. Your focus must be to build a solid rapport with the people. Always be punctual and transparent about everything in your interactions with the people. Your behavior will play an important role in establishing you as a brand.

If possible make some custom T-shirts with your hashtag and business name printed on it, make a habit to wear those while walking in dog parks. This may draw the attention of people towards your company, even if it doesn't, it would be wise to wear those for the purpose of branding.

Most of the business in the pet sitting industry usually comes from referrals. Whenever a customer is refereed to you, make sure to send those pictures of happy customers, or better still a video of a pet enjoying your company. Be punctual and strive to over-deliver in your promises. You can expect a decent increase in the business in a few months.

You can also build a geo-location app so that your customers can monitor your location in real time while you are taking care of their pet. This would provide a huge boost to the credibility of your business. This also shows your commitment and dedication to your work. This type of real-time monitoring creates a professional impression on the clients. This will differentiate you from other pet sitters and give your customers a sense of security and control over their pets. This also helps to ease any fears that the client might have if he is working for the first time with you. But technology can have its pros and cons. It is better to test the GPS software extensively, in different locations, in different weather because any upgrades in the operating systems or a bug can cause malfunctioning and can send adverse signals to the customer. While you may strive to provide the best user experience, it is better to monitor its performance on a weekly basis at least, GPS will become a norm in the near future with the advancement of technology, it could become an indispensable tool for pet sitting business. A GPS application can also send real-time notifications to the owners about their pets, and this ensures peace of mind for owners as well as pet sitters.

Other Books

From Broke To Bust – Step By Step Guide To Survive As Copywriter

www.ingramcontent.com/pod-product-compliance
Lightning Source LLC
Chambersburg PA
CBHW031516210526
45464CB00007B/2933